COSMOS QUESTIONS
WHAT CAUSES A SUPERNOVA?

by Clara MacCarald

pogo

Ideas for Parents and Teachers

Pogo Books let children practice reading informational text while introducing them to nonfiction features such as headings, labels, sidebars, maps, and diagrams, as well as a table of contents, glossary, and index.

Carefully leveled text with a strong photo match offers early fluent readers the support they need to succeed.

Before Reading

- "Walk" through the book and point out the various nonfiction features. Ask the student what purpose each feature serves.
- Look at the glossary together. Read and discuss the words.

During Reading

- Have the child read the book independently.
- Invite them to list questions that arise from reading.

After Reading

- Discuss the child's questions. Talk about how they might find answers to those questions.
- Prompt the child to think more. Ask: Did you know what supernovas were before reading this book? What more would you like to learn about them?

Pogo Books are published by Jump!
5357 Penn Avenue South
Minneapolis, MN 55419
www.jumplibrary.com

Copyright © 2026 Jump!
International copyright reserved in all countries.
No part of this book may be reproduced in any form without written permission from the publisher.

Jump! is a division of FlutterBee Education Group.

Library of Congress Cataloging-in-Publication Data

Names: MacCarald, Clara, 1979- author.
Title: What causes a supernova? / by Clara MacCarald.
Description: Minneapolis, MN: Jump!, Inc., [2026]
Series: Cosmos questions | Includes index.
Audience: Ages 7-10
Identifiers: LCCN 2024053605 (print)
LCCN 2024053606 (ebook)
ISBN 9798892138529 (hardcover)
ISBN 9798892138536 (paperback)
ISBN 9798892138543 (ebook)
Subjects: LCSH: Supernovae—Juvenile literature.
Stars—Juvenile literature.
Classification: LCC QB843.S95 (print)
LCC QB843.S95 (ebook)
DDC 523.8/4465—dc23/eng/20250213
LC record available at https://lccn.loc.gov/2024053605
LC ebook record available at https://lccn.loc.gov/2024053606

Editor: Alyssa Sorenson
Designer: Emma Almgren-Bersie

Photo Credits: Piysho/Shutterstock, cover; magann/iStock, 1; shufilm/Adobe Stock, 3, 12; m-gucci/iStock, 4; Thongsuk/Adobe Stock, 5; Goddard/SDO/NASA, 6-7; Josh/Adobe Stock, 8-9; ManowKem/Shutterstock, 10-11; Nechitayka/Shutterstock, 13; MARK GARLICK/SCIENCE PHOTO LIBRARY/Getty, 14-15; Lia Koltyrina/Shutterstock, 16-17tl; ART-ur/Shutterstock, 16-17tr; NASA ESA CSA STScl, 16-17 (bottom); Franco Tognarini/Shutterstock, 18; Vadimsadovski/Adobe Stock, 19; muratart/Shutterstock, 20-21; chathuporn/Adobe Stock, 23.

Printed in the United States of America at Corporate Graphics in North Mankato, Minnesota.

TABLE OF CONTENTS

CHAPTER 1
What Is a Star?...4

CHAPTER 2
Exploding Stars..12

CHAPTER 3
Studying Supernovas.......................................18

ACTIVITIES & TOOLS
Try This!..22
Glossary..23
Index...24
To Learn More..24

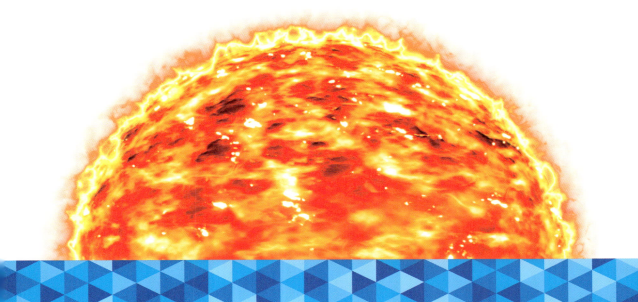

CHAPTER 1
WHAT IS A STAR?

Our **galaxy** has billions of stars. They twinkle in the night sky.

The Sun is a star. It is the closest star to Earth. It gives off heat and light. It makes life on our planet possible!

CHAPTER 1

A star is a huge ball of gas. It is mostly made of hydrogen and helium. These gases burn in a star's core, or center. This releases **energy**. It is how the star gives off heat and light.

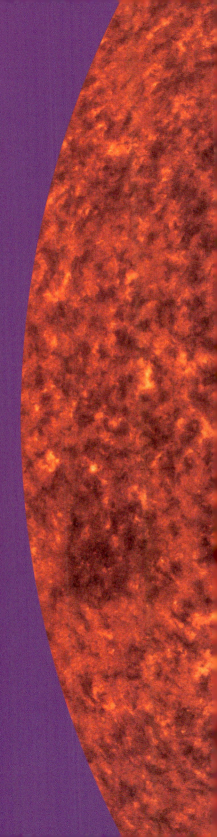

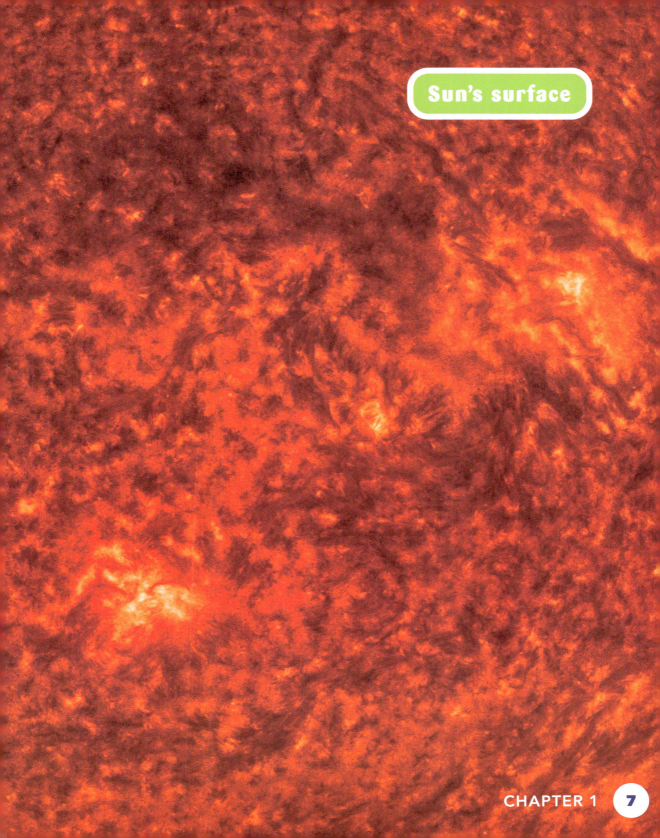

There are many types of stars. Blue stars are the hottest. Red stars are cooler. Some stars are bright. Others are dim. Stars are different sizes, too. White dwarfs are similar in size to Earth. Red and blue supergiants are large. Five billion Suns could fit inside a red supergiant!

red supergiant

CHAPTER 1

TAKE A LOOK!

How do stars compare? Take a look!

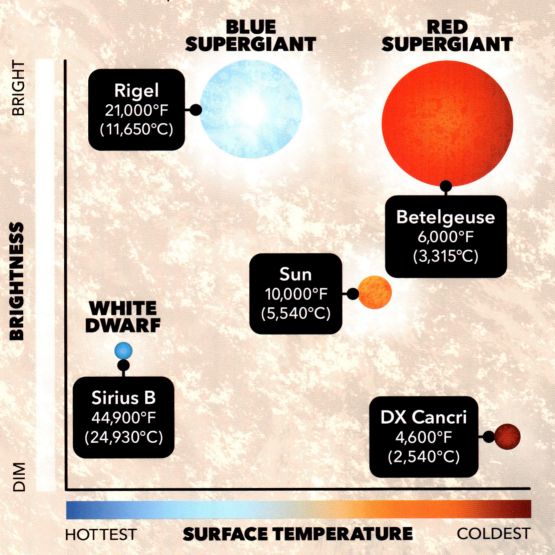

Stars are born from dust and gas. They move. They change. They can live trillions of years. Stars eventually run out of gases to burn. They die. Some stars blow up when this happens. This is called a supernova.

DID YOU KNOW?

Will the Sun die? Not in our lifetime. The Sun has 5 billion years of **fuel** left.

CHAPTER 1   11

CHAPTER 2
EXPLODING STARS

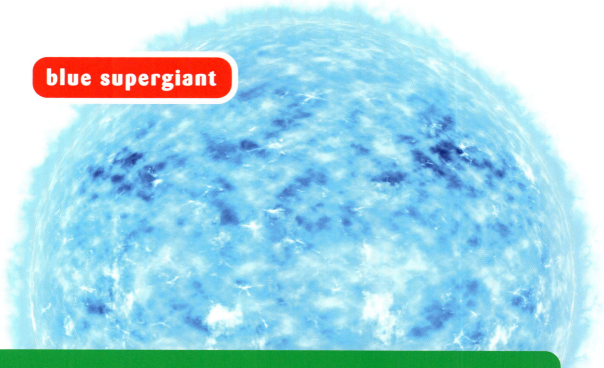

blue supergiant

Two types of stars have a supernova. The first is a large star. It must be at least eight times bigger than the Sun to explode into a supernova. Red supergiants and blue supergiants both die this way.

A large star runs out of fuel. It cannot hold its shape. Its **gravity** makes it fall in on itself. This happens in just a few seconds. It creates a supernova.

CHAPTER 2 13

white
dwarf

A white dwarf can have a supernova, too. This happens when a white dwarf is near a second star. Sometimes the white dwarf steals **matter** from the other star. Other times, a white dwarf and the other star crash into each other. In both cases, the result is a supernova.

DID YOU KNOW?

A supernova happens every 10 seconds.

CHAPTER 2   15

When stars explode, their cores often survive. They turn into something new. Some become **black holes**. Others become **neutron stars**. Gas and dust are left behind after an explosion. A **nebula** forms. New stars are made.

DID YOU KNOW?

Supernovas can create **elements**. Iron is one. We need iron to live. There is iron in your blood. It may be from a supernova!

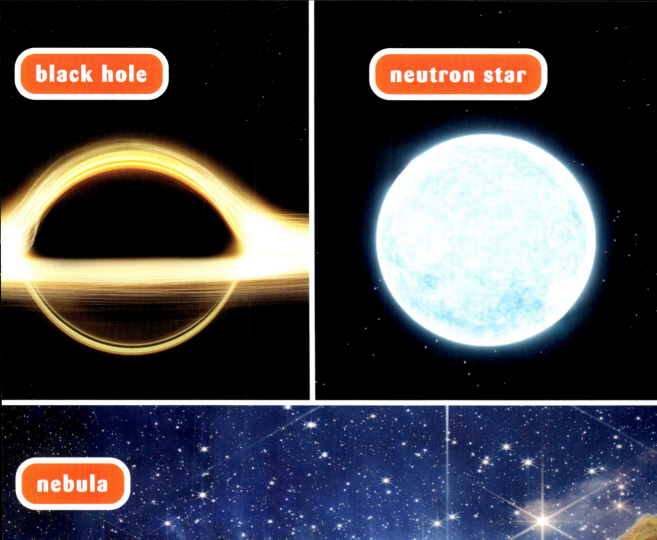

black hole

neutron star

nebula

CHAPTER 3

STUDYING SUPERNOVAS

Supernovas are huge and powerful. They give off a lot of light. The light may stay in the sky for months. Sometimes, if they are close, we can see the light with our own eyes!

supernova

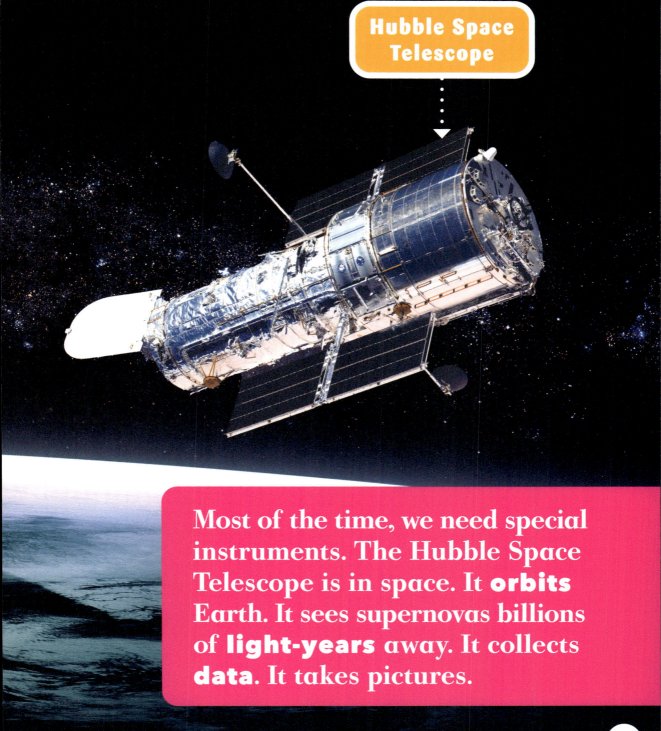

Hubble Space Telescope

Most of the time, we need special instruments. The Hubble Space Telescope is in space. It **orbits** Earth. It sees supernovas billions of **light-years** away. It collects **data**. It takes pictures.

CHAPTER 3 19

Scientists study them. Why? Supernovas tell us about our **universe**. They help us learn more about how galaxies are made. They tell us how galaxies change over time. They give us clues about how big our universe is!

ACTIVITIES & TOOLS

TRY THIS!

NEBULA IN A JAR

A nebula is a huge cloud of dust and gas. It has many different colors. Make your own nebula with this fun activity!

What You Need:
- water
- four bowls
- food coloring
- clear jar
- toothpick
- cotton balls
- glitter (optional)

1. Add water to the bowls. Put food coloring in each of the bowls. Make any colors you want.
2. Pour a layer of colored water into the jar. Add bits of cotton to the water. Press down with a toothpick until all the water is soaked up. You can add glitter at any point, too.
3. Add another layer of cotton. Pour a different color on top. Press down again, adding more cotton if needed.
4. Repeat until you have filled the jar. Enjoy your nebula!

GLOSSARY

black holes: Areas in space where stars have collapsed and where gravity is so strong that nothing can escape, not even light.

data: Information collected so something can be done with it.

elements: Substances that cannot be divided into simpler substances.

energy: The ability to do work.

fuel: Something used to produce energy.

galaxy: A very large group of stars and planets.

gravity: The force that pulls things toward the center of a space object and keeps them from floating away.

light-years: Measures of distance in space. One light-year is 5.9 trillion miles (9.5 trillion kilometers).

matter: Something that has weight and takes up space, such as a solid, liquid, or gas.

nebula: A huge cloud of gas and dust in space.

neutron stars: Dense objects in space that have closely packed neutrons and are made by the collapse of large stars.

orbits: Travels in a circular path around something.

universe: All existing matter and space.

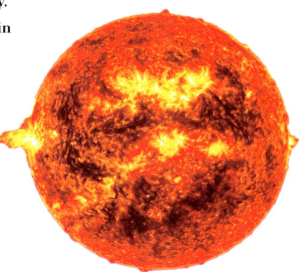

ACTIVITIES & TOOLS 23

INDEX

black holes 16
blue supergiant 8, 9, 12
burn 6, 11
core 6, 16
crash 15
data 19
Earth 5, 8, 19
elements 16
energy 6
fuel 11, 13
galaxy 4, 21
gas 6, 11, 16

gravity 13
Hubble Space Telescope 19
light-years 19
matter 15
nebula 16
neutron stars 16
orbits 19
planet 5
red supergiant 8, 9, 12
Sun 5, 8, 9, 11, 12
universe 21
white dwarfs 8, 9, 15

TO LEARN MORE

Finding more information is as easy as 1, 2, 3.
1. Go to www.factsurfer.com
2. Enter "supernova" into the search box.
3. Choose your book to see a list of websites.

24 ACTIVITIES & TOOLS